△ L I F E ' S ▲
little handbook of wisdom

△ L I F E ' S ▲
little handbook of wisdom

Bruce and Cheryl Bickel
Stan and Karin Jantz

A BARBOUR BOOK

Published by Barbour and Company, Inc.
            P.O. Box 719
            Uhrichsville, Ohio 44683

Typeset by Typetronix, Inc., Fort Myers, Florida

ISBN 1-55748-342-6 Graduate's Edition
ISBN 1-55748-386-8 Inspirational Library Edition

Printed in the United States of America

    2   3   4   5/ 98   97   96   95   94

△ L I F E ' S ▲
little handbook of wisdom

▲ Meet the Lord every morning.

❖

▲ Have a passion for God and compassion for people.

❖

▲ Choose the way of most persistence rather than the path of least resistance.

❖

▲ Friendships can fade. Family is forever.

❖

▲ What happens *in* you is more important than what happens *to* you.

❖

▲ Seek out quiet people. They have a lot to say if you say something first.

❖

▲ Fix the problem without fixing the blame.

❖

▲ Celebrate spiritual birthdays. If you don't know yours, arbitrarily select a date.

❖

▲ Pride is a disease that makes everyone sick except the person afflicted.

❖

▲ The way you live reflects your view of God.

❖

▲ It is never too late to make a change in your life.

▲ L I F E ' S △
little handbook of wisdom

▲ Freedom is doing what you know is right without fear.

❖

▲ Learn from the mistakes of others. You'll never live long enough to make them all yourself.

❖

▲ Pray for people you dislike.

❖

▲ Pray for people who dislike you.

❖

△ L I F E ' S ▲
little handbook of wisdom

▲ Prosperity is not always good, and adversity is not always bad.

❖

▲ Consider that whatever misfortune may be your lot, someone always has it worse than you — always.

❖

▲ If what you are doing won't make a difference in five years, it probably doesn't matter now.

❖

▲ Wall-to-wall carpeting isn't for everyone.

▲ Heed the advice of Orville Redenbacher: "Do one thing, and do it better than anyone."

❖

▲ Develop your vocabulary, but don't overuse fancy words.

❖

▲ Convince your kids there's more to life than fast food.

❖

△ L I F E ' S ▲
little handbook of wisdom

▲ Learn to laugh at yourself.

❖

▲ No television reporting is without bias.

❖

▲ Fly the flag on patriotic days.

❖

▲ Pray for your family every day.

❖

▲ Develop your own abilities while discovering the abilities of others.

❖

▲ Take your kids out for ice cream after they've performed in sports, drama, or music, especially if they didn't do very well.

❖

△ L I F E ' S ▲
little handbook of wisdom

▲ If you can't afford it, you don't need it.

❖

▲ Anything can last one more year.

❖

▲ Learn to tell a good story.

❖

▲ Live life on purpose, not by accident.

❖

▲ L I F E ' S △
little handbook of wisdom

▲   Read for fifteen minutes every night before you go to bed.

❖

▲   Read *How to Win Friends and Influence People* by Dale Carnegie at least once a year.

❖

▲   Rent movies you could watch with your mother in the room.

❖

△ **L I F E ' S** ▲
little handbook of wisdom

▲ Find a mentor.

❖

▲ Let your word be your bond:
    keep your promises;
    meet your deadlines;
    honor your commitments;
    pay your bills.

❖

▲ Encourage others to develop
their character by displaying yours.

❖

▲ Expect Christ's return.

❖

▲ Enjoy the journey as much as the destination.

❖

▲ Walk on soles, not on souls.

❖

▲ Develop your vocabulary to express yourself, not to impress others.

❖

△ L I F E ' S ▲
little handbook of wisdom

▲ Don't complain about the mud if you prayed for rain.

❖

▲ Give money to your church regularly.

❖

▲ Rent classic romance and comedy videos.

❖

▲ Be nice to the people who serve you.

❖

▲ L I F E ' S △
little handbook of wisdom

▲ Drive like you own the car, not the road.

❖

▲ Don't fall asleep at the wheel unless you're at the drive-in theater.

❖

▲ Treat your faith like a traveler's check: It can be accepted around the world!

❖

▲ Never criticize your barber while he's cutting your hair.

▲ Say "I love you" to your spouse at least once a day. Say it all the time with your eyes.

❖

▲ You'll know when something becomes meaningful to you when it goes from your head to your heart to your hands.

❖

▲ Next time you're in church, sit in the front row. You'll be amazed how much more you'll learn (not to mention how it will affect the preacher).

❖

▲ Eat until you're full, not stuffed.

❖

▲ Pray with perseverance and expectancy.

❖

▲ Check the batteries in your smoke detector. Now.

❖

▲ Plant some bulbs in your garden. You'll enjoy the flowers year after year.

❖

△ L I F E ' S ▲
little handbook of wisdom

▲ When you find a leader, follow.

❖

▲ When you identify a follower, lead.

❖

▲ Pick a passage or a chapter in the Bible and memorize it.

❖

▲ Watch an epic Bible movie with your family every year during Easter week.

❖

▲ Everybody has a life story. Think about yours, write it out, and then look for an opportunity to relate it publicly.

❖

▲ You can plan to succeed or you can plan to fail. The choice is yours.

❖

△ L I F E ' S ▲
little handbook of wisdom

▲ Don't wait for memories to happen. Plan them in advance.

❖

▲ Instead of dieting off and on, try eating less all the time.

❖

▲ Don't be obsessed with your weight. Good health is much more important than a single-digit dress size.

❖

▲ Enjoy happiness; treasure joy.

▲ L I F E ' S △
little handbook of wisdom

▲ Before you begin an extended car trip with your family, take a moment to pray together for safety.

❖

▲ Put loose change in a jar and save it.

❖

▲ Try to understand a person you are inclined to dislike.

❖

▲ Make New Year's resolutions—two or three times a year.

△ L I F E ' S ▲
little handbook of wisdom

▲ Be able to admit you are wrong.

❖

▲ Wisdom comes to those who seek it.

❖

▲ Dwelling on the honors you think you deserve may deny you the satisfaction of knowing you did your best.

❖

▲ Recognize that the perfect swimsuit may only be perfect from *one* angle.

▲ L I F E ' S △
little handbook of wisdom

▲ Memorize your social security number and the number on your driver's license.

❖

▲ Always do the job as if your boss were looking over your shoulder.

❖

▲ Don't establish a friendship based on mutual dislikes.

❖

▲ Recognize that you can't get holy in a hurry.

❖

▲ Decide, on a daily basis, not to complain.

❖

▲ Don't eat soup with a slotted spoon.

❖

▲ Complaining feeds the fuel of all irritations.

❖

▲ Plant a tree to commemorate a significant event. It will serve as a great reminder in future years.

❖

▲ When dealing with a difficult decision, seek good advice from others; then *you* make the decision.

❖

▲ What you *think* determines what you *do*.

❖

▲ Read the front page of a local newspaper every day. Keep up on current events.

▲ Be a reader, but one who reads between the lines.

❖

▲ Never let your yearnings exceed your earnings.

❖

▲ Be a friend to a lot of people.

❖

▲ Expose your children to live theatre or the symphony. They'll enjoy it now and appreciate it later.

❖

▲ Think back and remember one thing you really admired about your spouse when you were dating.

❖

△ L I F E ' S ▲
little handbook of wisdom

▲ It's okay to make a mistake.

❖

▲ Don't make the same mistake twice.

❖

▲ Prayer changes things.

❖

▲ Know your own strengths and weaknesses and work on them.

❖

▲ L I F E ' S △
little handbook of wisdom

▲ If you tend to fall asleep in church, sit in the back row. You can lean your head against the wall so it doesn't snap forward when you doze off.

❖

▲ Remember that God values you for *who* you are, not *what* you do.

❖

▲ Applaud all participants in a race, not just the winner.

❖

▲ Have lots of acquaintances and a few close friends.

▲ God is more interested in inner grace than in outer space.

❖

▲ You will have no greater joy than to hear that your children walk in truth.

❖

▲ The difference between mediocre and excellent is usually a very small amount of effort.

❖

▲ Discover your spiritual gifts. Then, get involved in a ministry so you can use them.

▲ L I F E ' S △
little handbook of wisdom

▲ If you want to be rich — give.

❖

▲ If you want to be poor — grasp.

❖

▲ If you want abundance — scatter.

❖

▲ If you want to be needy — hoard.

❖

▲ Love is forgiving and for giving.

❖

▲ Use a credit card only if you can pay the bill in full at the end of the month.

❖

▲ To belittle is to be little.

❖

▲ L I F E ' S △
little handbook of wisdom

▲ Asking makes the difference.

❖

▲ Be loyal to your spouse.
Express admiration in public.

❖

▲ Be one who says positive
things about others.

❖

▲ Make a list of six people you could count on to carry your casket at your funeral. If you can't come up with six, develop some new friendships, or plan to be cremated.

❖

▲ Read one book a month.

❖

▲ Reward your kids every time they read a book, even if it's for school.

❖

▲ L I F E ' S △
little handbook of wisdom

▲ When you travel, eat in local restaurants.

❖

▲ It's never been too long to renew an old friendship.

❖

▲ Look on the bright side.

❖

▲ Contentment with your situation breeds satisfaction.

❖

▲ L I F E ' S ▲
little handbook of wisdom

▲ In every situation, ask yourself, "What would Jesus do?" Then do it.

❖

▲ Associate with leaders as often as you can. When you're around them, carry a note pad and write things down.

❖

▲ Ask for advice often. Offer advice sparingly.

❖

▲ Let your difficulties be opportunities for God's control.

❖

▲ Discover your God-given abilities — then develop them.

❖

▲ Compliment your spouse with elegant words.

❖

△ L I F E ' S ▲
little handbook of wisdom

▲ Don't strain to hit the high notes.

❖

▲ Teach your kids responsibility early.

❖

▲ Never mistake activity for achievement.

❖

▲ Take the blame for your mistakes. Give God the credit for your successes.

❖

▲ Heed the advice you give to others.

❖

▲ Don't acquire everything you want.

❖

▲ Before you worry needlessly, ask yourself, "What's the worst thing that could happen?"

❖

△ L I F E ' S ▲
little handbook of wisdom

▲ Wear clothes that fit.

❖

▲ Never buy something for the purpose of impressing others.

❖

▲ Call your mother-in-law. Tell her how much you appreciate the person you married.

❖

▲ Instead of bringing your kids presents after a business trip, give them your time.

❖

▲ L I F E ' S △
little handbook of wisdom

▲ Develop an ear for music and
an eye for art.

❖

▲ Compliment men on their
ties.

❖

▲ Compliment women on their
shoes.

❖

▲ Smile at babies.

❖

△ **L I F E ' S** ▲
little handbook of wisdom

▲ Be a peacemaker.

❖

▲ Take your family out for breakfast on Saturdays.

❖

▲ Set aside money each month for vacations.

❖

▲ Set aside money each month for Christmas.

❖

▲ L I F E ' S △
little handbook of wisdom

▲ Take your kids to lunch on a regular basis.

❖

▲ When you feel like settling for less than the best, think about what God wants for you.

❖

▲ Always try to see the forest through the trees.

❖

▲ Your attitude is more important than your aptitude.

❖

▲ Make sure your decisions are based on pure motives.

❖

▲ When you have the choice between taking an escalator or the stairs, take the stairs.

❖

▲ If you act like you know
where you're going, you may end up
someplace you'd rather be anyway.

❖

▲ There's nothing wrong with
being average unless it's not your best.

❖

▲ At least once in your life
explore the crown jewels of the
National Park System: Yellowstone,
Yosemite, and the Grand Canyon.

❖

▲ If you don't have a Bible, get one.

❖

▲ If you've got a Bible, read it.

❖

▲ If you read the Bible, believe it.

❖

▲ If you believe the Bible, live it.

❖

▲ Develop priorities.

❖

▲ It's more important to listen
to another person's point of view than
to express your own.

❖

▲ Self-improvement is a life-
long process.

❖

▲ Your biggest success will be in striving to be the best you can be, and only you can succeed at that.

❖

▲ Don't waste your time trying to be like somebody else. Only they can do that.

❖

▲ Be happy for others in their good fortune.

❖

▲ L I F E ' S △
little handbook of wisdom

▲ Doing the right thing is always liberating.

❖

▲ Don't let the sands of time get in your lunch.

❖

▲ Criticism and finding fault are not spiritual gifts.

❖

▲ Read the instructions first. It's not much fun, but you'll save time in the long run.

❖

L I F E ' S
little handbook of wisdom

▲   There is a solution to every problem.

❖

▲   When you're feeling overwhelmed, remember to take things one at a time — one day at a time.

❖

▲   The line can often be busy when conscience wishes to speak.

❖

▲   Faith does not demand miracles, but often accomplishes them.

▲ Don't be so involved in the "when" that you miss the "now."

❖

▲ If you say you'll do it, DO IT!

❖

▲ Share your blessings with others.

❖

▲ If necessary, repeat yourself to emphasize your point.

❖

▲ If necessary, repeat yourself to emphasize your point.

❖

▲ Follow the promptings of your heart rather than the desires of your flesh.

❖

▲　Be honest with other people.

❖

▲　Be honest with yourself.

❖

▲　Motivations can fade. Habits prevail.

❖

▲　Stand up for someone who needs it.

❖

△ L I F E ' S ▲
little handbook of wisdom

▲ Don't be intimidated by your peers. God in you is always a majority.

❖

▲ Be as considerate with your family as you are with your friends.

❖

▲ Embrace your spouse.

❖

▲ Hug your kids.

❖

▲   Motivate, don't denigrate.

❖

▲   It doesn't take any extra time to be nice.

❖

▲   If you have to ask if something is right, it probably isn't.

❖

△ L I F E ' S ▲
little handbook of wisdom

▲ Avoid movies with the words "Dead," "Fatal," or "Hot" in the title.

❖

▲ Offer yourself as a friend to another. It will refresh both of you.

❖

▲ Make friends with someone of advanced years and let them know how much their friendship means.

❖

▲   Write down the name of your closest friend in the world. Now pick up a phone and place a call.

❖

▲   Fast and pray as often as you feast and play.

❖

▲   What the world sees we are, they consider Christ to be.

❖

▲ Our wealth is measured by
the fewness of our wants.

❖

▲ The best time to relax is
when you're too busy.

❖

▲ Don't be afraid to ask dumb
questions. Better a dumb question
than a dumb mistake.

❖

▲ Associate with people you can learn from.

❖

▲ Associate with people you can teach.

❖

▲ The person who does not read good books has no advantage over the one who can't read them.

❖

▲ Don't make plans and then ask for the Lord's approval. Ask the Lord to direct your planning.

❖

▲ If what you believe doesn't affect how you live, then it isn't very important.

❖

▲ Religion is man's attempt to find God. The Gospel is God's plan to reach man. Don't let religion stand in the way of your salvation.

❖

▲ L I F E ' S △
little handbook of wisdom

    ▲ Take control of your time.
Refuse to be lazy.

❖

    ▲ Stand up for something you
believe in.

❖

    ▲ Develop a unique style.

❖

    ▲ Always do more than is
expected of you. It will pay rich
rewards.

❖

△ L I F E ' S ▲
little handbook of wisdom

▲ You will never please everyone all of the time. Don't even try.

❖

▲ It's better to give your children experiences than things.

❖

▲ You don't need a house to have a home.

❖

▲ Sit with your family in church every week.

▲ Appreciate criticism. The comment may not hit the bull's-eye, but it will probably be on target.

❖

▲ Before you make a decision:
consider all the facts;
seek wise counsel;
pray.

❖

▲ If you want to go to sleep with a clear conscience, either live with integrity every day, or pray for forgiveness every night.

❖

△ L I F E ' S ▲
little handbook of wisdom

▲ Be flexible.

❖

▲ Remember, people don't look as critically at you as you look at yourself.

❖

▲ No one can hurt your feelings unless you let them.

❖

▲ Appreciate the differences in people you know. That's usually why you like them.

❖

▲ Little is much if God is in it.

❖

▲ Blow your own nose, but don't toot your own horn.

❖

△ L I F E ' S ▲
little handbook of wisdom

▲　Get involved at church.

❖

▲　When someone whispers a question to you, answer in a whisper.

❖

▲　Support a missionary financially.

❖

▲　Happiness comes not from having much to live on but from having much to live for.

❖

▲　Compliment people as soon as it occurs to you.

❖

▲　God is more likely to speak to you with a gentle whisper than with a loud voice.

❖

▲　Leave your boss' office two minutes before he or she asks you to.

❖

△ L I F E ' S ▲
little handbook of wisdom

▲ Be loyal to your friends.

❖

▲ Look people in the eye
when you talk to them.

❖

▲ Love is saying "no" when it's
easier to say "yes."

❖

▲ Love is being tender as a
kitten when you feel like a tiger.

❖

▲ Stand up when you hear the Word of God.

❖

▲ Bow down when you worship God.

❖

▲ Keep in shape.

❖

▲ When you feel insignificant, remember how important you are to God.

❖

△ L I F E ' S ▲
little handbook of wisdom

▲ Do something for someone without taking credit.

❖

▲ Be available to take someone's place in an emergency.

❖

▲ When you say you will pray for someone, DO IT.

❖

▲ Never expect gratitude, but always express appreciation.

❖

▲ The practice of honesty is more convincing than the profession of holiness.

❖

▲ Guide your kids.

❖

△ L I F E ' S ▲
little handbook of wisdom

▲ You are responsible for the depth of your spiritual understanding. God is responsible for the breadth of your ministry.

❖

▲ Love God, not godliness.

❖

▲ Plan one romantic getaway a year with your spouse.

❖

▲ L I F E ' S △
little handbook of wisdom

▲ Leave enthusiastic messages on answering machines and voice mail.

❖

▲ When you're feeling overwhelmed, make a list.

❖

▲ Think about your question before you ask it.

❖

△ L I F E ' S ▲
little handbook of wisdom

▲ Don't be afraid to try something you don't think you can do. You may surprise yourself and you'll probably enjoy it.

❖

▲ Ask other people about themselves.

❖

▲ If you find yourself in a questionable situation, get out immediately.

❖

▲ Good grooming will get you in the door. Good manners will get you past the foyer.

▲ L I F E ' S △
little handbook of wisdom

▲ Find your self worth in God's unconditional love for you, not in your accomplishments.

❖

▲ Adversity breeds genius: Don't give your kids everything they want, and when they're old enough, make them get a job.

❖

▲ Find peace by an open window, the breeze gently stirring the curtains.

❖

△ L I F E ' S ▲
little handbook of wisdom

▲ Read one of Paul's epistles each week and feel inspired. (When you finish, start over.)

❖

▲ Give classical music a try.

❖

▲ Watch the pennies and the dollars will take care of themselves.

❖

▲ L I F E ' S △
little handbook of wisdom

▲ The color of your socks should never be lighter than the color of your slacks.

❖

▲ If you do something wrong, admit it.

❖

▲ Someday all you will have is what you have given to God.

❖

▲ Live in such a way that when you die even the undertaker will be sad.

△ L I F E ' S ▲
little handbook of wisdom

▲ Set goals that are not easily within reach.

❖

▲ Trade in your car, not your spouse.

❖

▲ Listen with your eyes as well as your ears.

❖

▲ L I F E ' S △
little handbook of wisdom

▲ Associate with people who lift you up.

❖

▲ Disassociate yourself from people who pull you down.

❖

▲ Use your free time productively.

❖

▲ Learn to write fascinating letters.

❖

△ L I F E ' S ▲
little handbook of wisdom

▲ Call your parents on their birthdays.

❖

▲ Eat at least one meal a day together as a family.

❖

▲ Remember that God's will is not so much a function of time and place as it is an attitude of the heart.

❖

▲ Do the job assigned to you with excellence, and opportunity will find you.

▲ Always be on time.

❖

▲ Develop an outdoor exercise routine.

❖

▲ As you sit on a quiet beach, thank God for the ocean.

❖

▲ As you sit on a noisy beach, thank God for your Walkman.

❖

▲ No one can please God without adding a great deal of happiness to his or her own life.

❖

▲ God will never send a thirsty soul to a dry well.

❖

▲ Character is made by what you stand for; reputation by what you fall for.

❖

▲ L I F E ' S △
little handbook of wisdom

▲ Be efficient, but don't cut
corners.

❖

▲ If you want people to think
that you are interesting, ask them
questions about themselves.

❖

▲ Laugh *at* yourself. Laugh *with*
others.

❖

▲ Appreciate adversity.

❖

▲ Keep your car clean — it's a reflection of your self image.

❖

▲ When you're at a carwash and you see another car you admire, compliment the owner.

❖

▲ Call your mother — you know how she worries.

❖

▲ Send cards and notes to your grandparents on special occasions, and be sure to include current pictures of the family.

❖

▲ Exercise your nostrils. Smell the roses.

❖

▲ Be a leader — not a follower.

❖

△ L I F E ' S ▲
little handbook of wisdom

▲ If your outgo exceeds your income, your upkeep will be your downfall.

❖

▲ From every dollar you earn save some and tithe some.

❖

▲ Nothing is ever too small a thing to do when it is done for someone else.

❖

▲ A word spoken in anger cannot be erased. It plays over and over again.

▲   Satan can't make you an unbeliever, but he'll try to make you an ineffective one.

❖

▲   Busy people always have time for one more thing.

❖

▲   Even when a situation seems to be at its worst, give it two more weeks.

❖

▲ Give people the benefit of the doubt. They are usually not out to hurt you.

❖

▲ Have someone over on the spur of the moment.

❖

▲ Learn to play one sport with average skill.

❖

▲ There's always a job for one more person willing to do it well.

▲ Carry a spare tire (in your car trunk, not around your waist).

▲ Live the Christian life as if the Lord were guiding your steps.

△ L I F E ' S ▲
little handbook of wisdom

▲ Learn about nutrition: feed your body healthy foods.

❖

▲ Study the Bible: feed your soul spiritual food.

❖

▲ Give the gift of time. It's a gift more valuable than money can buy.

❖

▲   If you don't stand for something, you'll fall for anything.

❖

▲   Love yourself as the unique individual God created you to be — nothing more, nothing less.

❖

▲   Learn to thrive on challenge and change.

❖

▲ Plan to be spontaneous.

❖

▲ Make sure your caring
includes doing.

❖

▲ Be polite to the panhandler.

❖

▲ L I F E ' S △
little handbook of wisdom

▲ Be as enthusiastic to stay married as you were to get married.

❖

▲ Direction is more important than speed.

❖

▲ Share your time but not your toothbrush.

❖

▲ Be the first one to ask a question.

❖

△ **L I F E ' S** ▲
little handbook of wisdom

▲   Remember, there is a time for love and a place for love. Any time, any place.

❖

▲   A testimony is better than a title.

❖

▲   Strive to be a person of faith rather than fame.

❖

▲ True communication begins when two people pray together.

❖

▲ Make it a goal to always make good on your promises, no matter how long it takes.

❖

▲ To love God is to obey God.

❖

▲ If you want to achieve excellence, begin with discipline.

❖

▲ At the beginning of each year, choose a topic of interest and spend the next twelve months learning all you can about it.

❖

▲ *Pray* as if the task depends on God and *work* as if it depends on you.

❖

▲ Learn the proper names of the trees in your yard.

❖

▲ Read at least one biography a year.

❖

▲ Keep fresh flowers in your home.

❖

▲ Develop a cause for your life. Whatever it is, dedicate yourself to it daily.

❖

△ **L I F E ' S** ▲
little handbook of wisdom

▲ Be a person of principle, passion, and purity.

▲ Make an appointment with God every day and then keep it as if you were meeting with the most important person in the world.

▲ Focus on your abilities rather than your limitations.

▲ Be cautious in telling others what you can do, but be bold in asserting what God can do.

❖

▲ Satisfaction begins when comparison stops.

❖

▲ Whenever you feel insignificant, remember how important you are to God.

❖

▲ Significance is found not in the quantity of work attempted, but in the quality of work accomplished.

❖

▲ The antidote to self-doubt is a dynamic belief in God.

❖

▲ If faced with a "take it or leave it" decision, you better leave it.

❖

▲ Long-term relationships are hard to establish and even harder to break. Choose them carefully.

❖

▲ If you want to be known as a trustworthy person, consistently back your words with action.

❖

▲ Memorize the names of the Seven Dwarfs.

❖

△ L I F E ' S ▲
little handbook of wisdom

▲ If you're going to wait for someone, wait for the Lord.

❖

▲ Take a little more than your share of the blame.

❖

▲ Take a little less than your share of the credit.

❖

▲ Life will be easier when you realize how hard it is.

❖

▲ You can still be a role model even if you're less than a model parent.

❖

▲ Make your home a place where your kids can bring their friends.

❖

▲ Make moments of stillness, quiet, and solitude part of your daily routine.

❖

▲ There are those who dream and those who do and those who do both. Join the third group.

❖

▲ Feeling good about yourself begins with serving others.

❖

▲ Next time you visit your grandparents, bring a video camera and record their memories.

❖

▲ God will either protect you from hardship or give you the strength to go through it. You win either way.

❖

▲ If you want to build a life of spiritual leadership, begin with a foundation of prayer.

❖

▲ Before you can ask integrity of others, you must attempt to be blameless yourself.

❖

△ L I F E ' S ▲
little handbook of wisdom

▲ It's easier to make a promise than to make good on one.

❖

▲ Clear summer nights are perfect for camping out in the backyard; taking walks; laying on a blanket and gazing at the stars; and driving with the windows rolled down.

❖

▲ For once, resist navy blue.

❖

▲ Hold on to friendships tightly;
release possessions easily.

❖

▲ Spontaneity is most effective
when it's planned in advance.

❖

▲ Keep a guest book in your
home.

❖

▲ Discipline begins with small
things done daily.

❖

△ L I F E ' S ▲
little handbook of wisdom

▲ Consistency works better when it's linked to persistency.

❖

▲ Instead of valuing something by its cost, figure out how much it's worth.

❖

▲ If time is more valuable than money, carefully plan how you spend it.

❖

▲ Once in a while, set a goal
that absolutely scares you.

❖

▲ Never underestimate your
opponent.

❖

▲ A dynamic life begins with
knowledge and culminates in love.

❖

L I F E ' S
little handbook of wisdom

▲ Teach a Sunday school class at least once a year.

❖

▲ What you *are* bears little resemblance to what you *have*.

❖

▲ God's anger lasts only a moment, but His favor lasts a lifetime.

❖

▲ L I F E ' S △
little handbook of wisdom

▲ Live independently of people's opinions of you.

❖

▲ Life is too short to buy green bananas.

❖

▲ Underpromise and overdeliver.

❖

△ L I F E ' S ▲
little handbook of wisdom

▲ Study your own behavior.

❖

▲ Do not pretend to know
when all you can offer is a guess.

❖

▲ Look in the mirror before
you leave home, never after.

❖

▲   Anything in basic black is back.

❖

▲   Failing to respond to a negative comment about someone else implies your agreement.

❖

▲   Choosing not to respond to a criticism about you shows strength of character.

❖

▲ Avoid making statements that can be taken two ways.

❖

▲ Know what God expects of you. If you don't know, look it up in the Bible.

❖

▲ Sometimes life is like dancing with a gorilla: You're not done until the gorilla is.

❖

▲   Claim no grace that is not yours, but possess all the grace available in Christ.

❖

▲   Humility grows out of strength. Pride grows out of weakness.

❖

▲   Make it your constant goal to be obedient, not victorious.

❖

▲ You will begin to live when you lose yourself in God's purpose for you.

❖

▲ Recognition is good; admiration is better.

❖

▲ Spend more of your time, energy, and resources investing in people than you do investing in things.

❖

▲ Make it a habit to get up an hour earlier than anyone else in your house.

❖

▲ Let your eating be guided more by health than by appetite.

❖

▲ Be quick to receive the truth, and even quicker to dismiss gossip.

❖

▲   Generosity does not include giving away something you'll never miss.

❖

▲   Generosity begins by giving yourself to God.

❖

▲   Sometime in the next month, try giving the Lord a day out of your life. An entire day.

❖

▲ If you maintain important relationships, they're less likely to require repairs.

❖

▲ Use superlatives sparingly.

❖

▲ Be aware of your own body language when listening or speaking.

❖

▲ If you're going to compare yourself to anyone, compare yourself to Christ. It will put your life in perspective.

❖

▲ True love is more an act of your will than a product of your emotions.

❖

▲ Buy a new Christmas recording each year.

❖

▲ Call your pastor and tell him how much you appreciate him.

❖

▲ Commit yourself to projects; dedicate yourself to people.

❖

▲ Take the family camping at least once a year.

△ L I F E ' S ▲
little handbook of wisdom

▲ Keep a family photo album up to date.

❖

▲ The next rainy day show your kids their baby pictures.

❖

▲ Take a tour of your state capital.

❖

▲ Always exercise your right to vote. Always.

❖

▲ Don't complain about travail if you prayed for patience.

❖

▲ Rejoice in the Lord's discipline as well as His blessings.

❖

△ L I F E ' S ▲
little handbook of wisdom

▲ Before diving into anything,
step back and view the big picture.

❖

▲ It's better to run behind God
than in front of Him.

❖

▲ Listen to books on tape
when you take extended car trips.

❖

▲ Imitate your life insurance agent: Be systematic about sending birthday cards to people who are important to you.

❖

▲ Everybody makes mistakes; not everyone learns from them.

❖

▲ Keep your promises, even when it hurts.

❖

△ L I F E ' S ▲
little handbook of wisdom

▲ Make a daily habit to read the chapter in Proverbs that corresponds to the current date.

❖

▲ Make friends even if you don't think you need them.

❖

▲ Roast marshmallows over a campfire.

❖

▲ L I F E ' S △
little handbook of wisdom

▲ If you want to lead, read.

❖

▲ Be satisfied with what you don't have as well as with what you do.

❖

▲ Get to know your intuitions.

❖

▲ Learn to relax without feeling guilty.

❖

▲ Faith is not an emotion. It is objective trust placed in a very real God.

❖

▲ If you want to know what's in your heart, listen to your mouth.

❖

▲ When you develop your film, get double prints. Give the duplicates away.

❖

▲ God won't take away a sin until you give it over to Him.

❖

▲ Broken relationships are best restored by forgiveness. If there is someone who needs your forgiveness, don't hold it back.

❖

△ L I F E ' S ▲
little handbook of wisdom

▲ When in the presence of others, don't put your hands on any part of your body that is covered.

❖

▲ Keep your fingernails trimmed. A person's hands tell much about them.

❖

▲ Don't talk when you are yawning; don't yawn while someone else is talking.

❖

▲ People are attracted to enthusiasm.

❖

▲ Write a thank-you note to a Sunday school teacher from your past.

❖

▲ When given the choice between two evils, don't choose either of them.

❖

▲ Select friends based on their character, not their compliments.

△ L I F E ' S ▲
little handbook of wisdom

▲ Don't be afraid to ask.

❖

▲ Have your next goal in mind before you achieve the one you are working on.

❖

▲ When you can, walk.

❖

▲ Don't worry so much about where you *are* as where you are *going*.

❖

▲ You should always believe what you say, but you don't always need to say what you think.

❖

▲ Make your home a place where people feel welcome.

❖

▲ God may be using people who disagree with you.

❖

▲ Visit the Vietnam Memorial Wall in Washington, D.C.

▲ As a Christian, you are designed and equipped to change the world for God's glory.

❖

▲ You learn more by listening. (You already know what you would say.)

❖

▲ Don't worry about proving God's existence because no one can disprove it.

❖

▲ Don't let your dreams die.

▲ Keep your financial affairs in order and discard useless paperwork. Remember that someone will be looking through your files when you die.

❖

▲ The same principle applies to your underwear drawer.

❖

▲ Eat slowly.

❖

▲ Pray for your mayor and local government officials.

△ **L I F E ' S** ▲
little handbook of wisdom

▲　Respect the environment.

❖

▲　Don't eat between meals,
and don't have more than three
ample meals a day.

❖

▲　If you are in an exchange of
harsh words with a friend, have thick
skin and a short memory.

❖

▲　Realize your inadequacy
without God and your sufficiency with
God.

▲ Find a good accountant, lawyer, doctor, and hair stylist. Only take advice from your hair stylist if it's about your hair.

❖

▲ Find a gentle dentist with an even gentler hygienist..

❖

▲ Feeling sorry for someone is okay; helping them is better.

❖

▲ A decision may not get easier with delay.

▲　Don't get into a stinking contest with a skunk.

❖

▲　Make God's provision the foundation for your performance.

❖

▲　Don't be good at making excuses.

❖

▲　Call if you're running late.

❖

▲ Manage your money as if it belongs to God. It does.

❖

▲ Try not to forget to. . .

❖

▲ Never play leapfrog with a rhinoceros.

❖

▲ Know when to choose between giving someone a pat on the back or a kick in the pants.

❖

▲ Keep a selection of greeting cards on hand so you'll have one on the spur of the moment.

❖

▲ Whenever possible, word your criticism in the form of a challenge.

❖

▲ To find out your priorities in life, look at your excesses.

❖

▲ Take out the trash before the garbage truck is two houses away.

❖

▲ Don't confuse doing things with accomplishing things.

❖

▲ Compliment a bald man on his smile.

❖

▲ Stand still, silent, and with your hand over your heart when the American flag passes by.

❖

▲ It is hard to learn from a mistake you don't acknowledge making.

❖

▲ Prefer one bird in the hand to two birds overhead.

❖

▲ If you agree to bury the hatchet, don't leave the handle sticking out.

❖

▲ Everybody makes mistakes — learn from theirs as well as your own.

❖

▲ Everybody makes mistakes; not everyone learns from them.

❖

▲ Thank God that your salvation does not depend on you.

❖

▲ Plan your funeral (but don't plan on attending).

❖

▲ If doctrine is your motivation, you will be a fanatic; if God is your motivation, you will be an obedient servant.

❖

▲ Understand the difference between acting young and being immature.

❖

▲ The parents' role is not to make all the right choices for their children, but to teach them how to make those choices for themselves.

❖

▲ Have a best friend who can multiply your joy and divide your sorrow.

❖

▲ We can't always choose the situations that life brings us, but we can choose the attitude we will use to face them.

❖

▲ Always leave the campsite cleaner than you found it.

❖

▲ Be willing to do today what others will not do, so that you can do tomorrow what others cannot do.

❖

▲ L I F E ' S △
little handbook of wisdom

▲ A modest person may not be noticed at first but will be respected later.

❖

▲ Hold to your opinions in such a way than you can change them. Let your convictions hold you in such a way that they affect your life.

❖

▲ Let your kids develop their own style.

❖

▲ Don't insult the IRS agent until the audit is concluded. Even then, don't do it.

❖

▲ Never be ashamed of your faith.

❖

▲ If your knees are knocking, kneel on them.

❖

▲   You'll miss your opportunities if you're too busy looking for a sure thing.

❖

▲   Write the elected officials who represent you on a regular basis. Tell them what you think.

❖

▲   Appreciate the commands of Scripture as much as the promises.

❖

△ L I F E ' S ▲
little handbook of wisdom

▲   A card sent with a personal note inside is so much more meaningful than a card sent but only signed.

❖

▲   You can give without loving, but you can't love without giving.

❖

▲   Ask the Lord to teach you His ways.

❖

▲ Suppress neither sneezes nor laughter.

❖

▲ Your care for others is a measure of your greatness.

❖

▲ As you go through the day, look for opportunities too good to miss.

❖

▲ Give thanks before each meal.

△ L I F E ' S ▲
little handbook of wisdom

▲ Remember to ask friends to pray for your needs.

❖

▲ Have a ready smile and a firm handshake.

❖

▲ "Holier than thou" refers to no one human.

❖

▲ The person who often looks up to God rarely looks down on anyone.

▲ Always go the extra mile . . . whether for a friend or chocolate mint chip ice cream.

❖

▲ "I'm sorry." Two words with unlimited potential.

❖

▲ Visit the Holy Land one time in your life.

❖

▲ Know all the words to a favorite hymn. Don't be hymn-nil.

▲ Staying within the lines is a lesson in coloring and patience.

▲ Wear a watch and be aware of appointments.

▲ Know how you stand with God. If you don't, join or start a small group with whom you can share your spiritual and personal concerns.

▲ Remember those who are alone, especially on holidays.

❖

▲ Give your spouse a gift for no reason.

❖

▲ With each passing year, be thankful for the richer complexity of the fabric of your life.

❖

▲ Learn to read music.

▲ Dine by candlelight at least once a week.

❖

▲ Unconditional love comes only from our Heavenly Father. And, if we're lucky, our parents.

❖

▲ The best jokes are painless, *and* profaneless.

❖

▲ Our five senses are incomplete without the sixth — a sense of humor.

▲ L I F E ' S △
little handbook of wisdom

▲ Check out magazines from
the library.

❖

▲ Know when to say goodbye.

❖

▲ Keep a Bible by your bed and
join the Lord each evening.

❖